BULGARIA

...in Pictures

Courtesy of Balkan Holidays

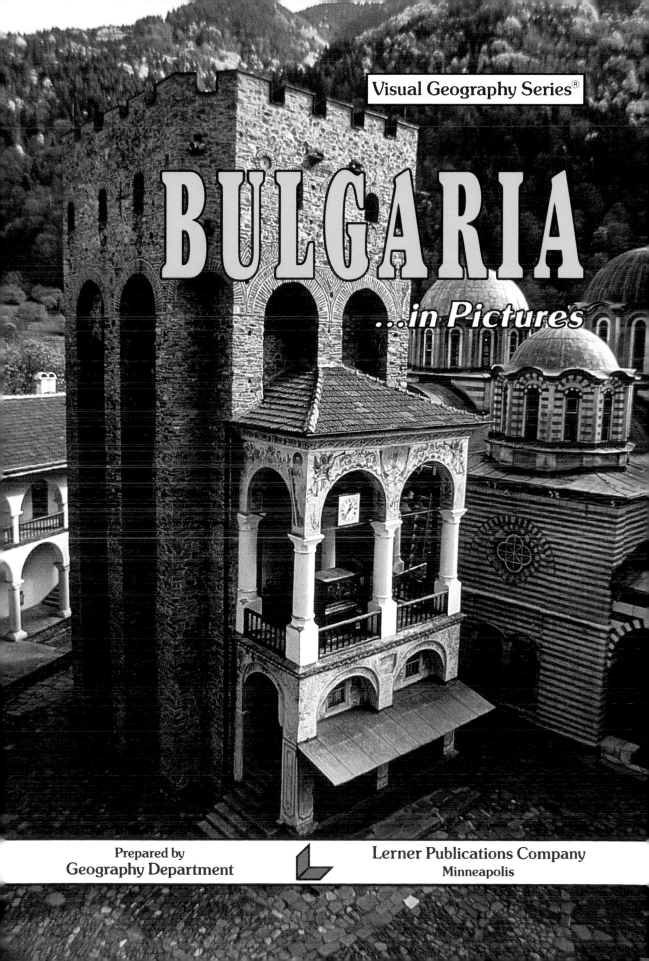

Visual Geography Series®

BULGARIA

...in Pictures

Prepared by
Geography Department

Lerner Publications Company
Minneapolis

Independent Picture Service

This popular resort hotel on Bulgaria's Black Sea coast once welcomed the visiting monarchs of Europe.

This book is an all-new edition of the Visual Geography Series. Previous editions were published by Sterling Publishing Company, New York City. The text, set in 10/12 Century Textbook, is fully revised and updated, and new photographs, maps, charts, and captions have been added.

LIBRARY OF CONGRESS CATALOGING-IN-PUBLICATION DATA

Bulgaria in pictures / prepared by Geography Department, Lerner Publications Company.
    p.   cm. – (Visual geography series)
    Includes index.
    Summary: Describes the topography, history, economy, society, and culture of the country situated on the Balkan Peninsula in southeastern Europe.
    ISBN 0-8225-1890-2 (lib. bdg.)
    1. Bulgaria—Juvenile literature. [1. Bulgaria.]
I. Lerner Publications Company. Geography Dept.
II. Series: Visual geography series (Minneapolis, Minn.)
DK510.56.B85   1994
949.77 – dc20   93-23080
                                        CIP
                                        AC

International Standard Book Number: 0-8225-1890-2
Library of Congress Catalog Card Number: 93-23080

VISUAL GEOGRAPHY SERIES®

Publisher
Harry Jonas Lerner
Senior Editor
Mary M. Rodgers
Editors
Gretchen Bratvold
Tom Streissguth
Colleen Sexton
Photo Researcher
Erica Ackerberg
Editorial/Photo Assistant
Marybeth Campbell
Consultants/Contributors
Ekaterina Ognianova
Sandra K. Davis
Designer
Jim Simondet
Cartographer
Carol F. Barrett
Indexer
Sylvia Timian
Production Manager
Gary J. Hansen

Photo © David and Cathy Memmott

A Bulgarian shepherd tends a flock gathered from the local villagers. He will return the sheep to their owners at the end of the day.

Acknowledgments

Title page photo © David and Cathy Memmott.

Elevation contours adapted from *The Times Atlas of the World,* seventh comprehensive edition (New York: Times Books, 1985).

1 2 3 4 5 6 – I/JR – 99 98 97 96 95 94

Rowboats, water taxis, and fishing vessels line the shore of the Black Sea, which forms a long coastline in eastern Bulgaria. Many of Bulgaria's ports were founded by the ancient Greeks, who used them as trading links to cities on the Balkan Peninsula.

Contents

ROMANIA

Danube R.

Kozlodui

Ruse

Tulenovo

Iskur R.

Pleven

Pliska
(Ruins)

Varna

Vratsa

Lovech

Preslav

SERBIA

Veliko Turnovo

Kamchiya R.

Gabrovo

Kremikovtsi

Nesebur

SOFIA

Kazanluk

Pernik

Lake
Iskur

Burgas

Gulf of Burgas

Struma R.

Hisarya

BLACK
SEA

Rila Monastery

Plovdiv

Maritsa R.

MACEDONIA

Sandanski

Mesta R.

Melnik

TURKEY

GREECE

BULGARIA

N

Province and City
Boundaries

Major Roads

AEGEAN SEA

| 0 | 20 | 40 | 60 | Miles |
| 0 | 20 | 40 | 60 | Kilometers |

EUROPE
BULGARIA

20° 0° 20°

Arctic Circle

NORWEGIAN
SEA

| 0 | 400 | Miles |
| 0 | 400 | Kilometers |

60°   60°

NORTH
ATLANTIC
OCEAN

20°

40°

MEDITERRANEAN SEA

0°   20°   40°

METRIC CONVERSION CHART
To Find Approximate Equivalents

WHEN YOU KNOW:	MULTIPLY BY:	TO FIND:
AREA		
acres	0.41	hectares
square miles	2.59	square kilometers
CAPACITY		
gallons	3.79	liters
LENGTH		
feet	30.48	centimeters
yards	0.91	meters
miles	1.61	kilometers
MASS (weight)		
pounds	0.45	kilograms
tons	0.91	metric tons
VOLUME		
cubic yards	0.77	cubic meters
TEMPERATURE		
degrees Fahrenheit	0.56 (*after* subtracting 32)	degrees Celsius

Photo by Dick Doughty

Crowds make way for a colorful parade during the annual Rose Festival in Kazanluk. During the spring, factories in this central Bulgarian city process freshly picked rose petals into attar of roses, a valuable perfume oil.

Introduction

Bulgaria, a country of nine million people, lies on the Balkan Peninsula of south-eastern Europe. For more than 40 years, Bulgaria was a member of the Communist bloc, a group of nations closely linked to the Soviet Union. The Communist party of Bulgaria ruled the country by taking control of agriculture and industry and by banning opposing political parties. In 1990 Bulgarians ended their Communist regime and established a new, democratic republic.

Settled in the sixth and seventh centuries by Bulgars and Slavs, Bulgaria grew to become the most powerful state in the Balkans. But in the late fourteenth century, the Ottoman (Turkish) Empire conquered Bulgaria and much of south-eastern Europe. Bulgarians lived under complete domination by the Turks until the 1800s, when the Ottoman Empire began to weaken. A war of liberation, in which Russia supplied soldiers and weapons to the Bulgarians, broke out in 1876. The gradual withdrawal of the Turks from Europe allowed Bulgaria to establish complete independence in 1908.

During World War II (1939–45), the Soviet Union—which included Russia—imposed Communist regimes on Bulgaria and on several other European nations.

Independent Picture Service

Steep sandstone cliffs rise on the outskirts of Melnik, one of Bulgaria's smallest towns.

After the Bulgarian Communist government seized power, the Soviets provided money and raw materials to help develop Bulgaria's economy. Industrialization, as well as better health care and education, gradually improved the nation's standard of living. Bulgaria remained a loyal Soviet ally during the 1950s and 1960s, a period when people in many other Soviet-bloc nations defied their own Communist leaders.

Yet economic problems and political unrest eventually brought down Bulgaria's Communist party. The new government, which has been in power since 1990, has moved away from a centrally planned economy and towards a free-market system. Although most Bulgarians support this policy, the process of rebuilding the nation's economy will be long and difficult.

Photo by Bernice K. Condit

In 1969, when Bulgaria was under Communist control, the government posted photographs of Communist leaders along a busy street in Plovdiv, Bulgaria's second largest city.

Bulgaria stands at a historical crossroads, where Turkish, Slavic, and other cultures influenced the nation's art and society. The architect of these nineteenth-century apartments in Lovech used a style popular in the central European realm of Austria-Hungary.

1) The Land

Bulgaria is located in a mountainous region with a long history of conflict. Turkey and Greece, ancient rivals, lie south and southeast of Bulgaria, respectively. The republics of Macedonia and Serbia, Bulgaria's western neighbors, gained their independence after the violent breakup of Yugoslavia in the early 1990s.

North of Bulgaria is Romania, and to the east, along a 175-mile coastline, is the Black Sea. Bulgaria's total area of 42,823 square miles makes the country about the size of Tennessee. The greatest distance from north to south is 170 miles. East to west, Bulgaria stretches 306 miles at its widest point.

Topography

Rugged mountain ranges dominate Bulgaria, where the average elevation exceeds 1,500 feet above sea level. Between the mountains are narrow river valleys and densely populated plains. These areas

Photo © David and Cathy Memmott

Although Bulgaria is a small country, its mountain ranges, river valleys, plains, and long seacoast offer a great variety of landscapes. Over time, wind and water have eroded these hills near Melnik.

benefit from fertile land and a mild climate.

The Danube Plateau, with the country's lowest average elevation, extends across northern Bulgaria. Tributaries of the Danube River flow north through narrow valleys in the plateau. The fertile soil of the region allows farmers to grow grain and other food crops.

To the south, the valleys and plains of the Danube Plateau gradually slope upward to meet the Balkan Mountains, or Stara Planina, meaning "old mountains" in the Bulgarian language. This range runs across the country and reaches its highest point at Botev Peak (7,795 feet). Within the Balkan Mountains is the Shipka Pass, the site of a famous nineteenth-century battle between Bulgarian and Turkish troops. The Iskur Gorge in the west leads to the Bulgarian capital of Sofia. Mount Vitosha, just south of the city, is a familiar landmark to Sofia residents.

South of the main Balkan range is the Sredna Gora (middle forest). This wooded ridge is about 100 miles long and climbs to 5,000 feet in height. Between the Balkan Mountains and the Sredna Gora lies the narrow Valley of Roses. Here farmers grow flowers for processing into a fragrant oil known as attar of roses.

The southern slopes of the Sredna Gora gradually descend to the Thracian Plain, a region of hills and lowlands stretching along the valleys of the Maritsa River and its tributaries. East of the Maritsa valley rise the Sakar Mountains. The flat Burgas Lowland, an extension of the Thracian Plain, reaches the Black Sea coast.

The Rhodope Mountains, which dominate southwestern Bulgaria, feature rocky peaks, steep gorges, and a few freshwater lakes. The Rhodope range includes the rugged Rila Mountains south of Sofia and the Pirin Mountains, which run to Bulgaria's border with Greece. Musala Peak,

Historic churches, monasteries, and fortresses—many of them unused and uninhabited for centuries—dot the countryside. In remote areas, these structures provided shelter for Bulgarians during periods of war and foreign occupation.

the highest point on the Balkan Peninsula, reaches 9,597 feet within the Rila Mountains.

Rivers

Bulgaria has many small, fast-moving streams and rivers that flow from highland areas down to the valleys and lowlands. North of the Balkan Mountains, rivers run northward to the Danube or eastward to the Black Sea. Waterways south of the Balkan and Rila mountains cross the Greek border and empty into the Aegean Sea.

Photo © David and Cathy Memmott

Photo by Anne-Marie Hupchick and Dennis P. Hupchick

At Belogradchik Rocks, in northwestern Bulgaria, the ancient Romans built a stronghold that included these unusual towers of stone. The weirdly shaped rock formations have inspired many colorful names, including the Dog Rock, the Sphinx, the Bears, and the Elephant Rock.

11

The construction of a large dam created this lake in the Rhodope Mountains. The lake provides a freshwater environment for carp, which a local fish-farming operation raises and harvests.

The Danube River, which forms most of Bulgaria's long border with Romania, is the country's only navigable waterway. Many cargo ships carrying grain, coal, and industrial goods travel the Danube and call at the Bulgarian port of Ruse. Although the Danube is at least a mile wide along its lower course, floods in spring and a month of winter ice slow the busy river traffic.

Barges navigate the Danube River, which measures one mile across along the Bulgarian border. Bulgaria ships many of its products to foreign markets via the Danube.

The largest tributary of the Danube is the Iskur, which rises in the Rila Mountains, cuts a pass through the Balkan range, and then flows northeastward through the Danube Plateau. The Kamchiya River, in the eastern Balkan Mountains, reaches the Black Sea at the port of Varna.

The source of the Maritsa River, the main waterway of the Thracian Plain, lies high in the Rila Mountains. Cities, villages, and farms dot the broad Maritsa valley. After leaving Bulgaria, the Maritsa forms the border between Greece and Turkey before emptying into the Aegean Sea. The Struma and Mesta rivers tumble down steep mountain gorges in southwestern Bulgaria and flow southward into Greece.

Bulgaria's waterways have played an important role in the country's development. Pumping stations drain water directly from the Danube for irrigation. Several large reservoirs created by river dams also provide water for crops and for use in large cities. Dams on the rapid upper courses of the Iskur and Struma rivers supply hydroelectric power.

Climate

Bulgaria's climate varies greatly among mountain ranges, river valleys, plains, and coastal lowlands. In general, the northern half of the country has greater temperature extremes, while southern Bulgaria enjoys more sunshine and a longer growing season.

Winds from the north and east sweep across the Danube Plateau, which has hot summers and cold winters. The mountains that surround Sofia block these winds, but the capital's high elevation causes colder winters than in the Bulgarian lowlands. In January, the coldest month, temperatures

Photo by Anne-Marie Hupchick and Dennis P. Hupchick

A winter snowstorm has blanketed a rural cottage near Musala Peak, the highest point on the Balkan Peninsula. Snow covers some highland areas of Bulgaria throughout the year.

A small tributary of the Struma River rushes past a wooded hillside in the Pirin Mountains, near Bulgaria's border with Greece. This part of southwestern Bulgaria supports abundant wildlife and natural forests.

peaks are capped by snow during most of the year. The entire country receives an annual average of 25 inches of precipitation, most of which falls in the early summer. Drought is common, however, in the late summer.

Flora and Fauna

Bulgaria remained mostly rural and agricultural until the middle of the twentieth century, and extensive natural forests have survived the country's industrialization. Woodlands still cover about one-third of Bulgarian territory. Evergreen and deciduous (leaf-shedding) trees, including beech and oak, thrive in the Rhodope Mountains. Mixed forests also cover the lower slopes of the Balkan Mountains. Hardy pines and firs grow as far as the tree line (the level above which the soil and climate will not sustain trees).

Walnut and chestnut trees are common in the valley of the Maritsa River. Lianas, flowering trees, and other subtropical plants exist along the rivers of the Burgas Lowland and on the Black Sea coast. Bulgaria also has wild apple, pear, and plum trees in areas with a mild climate and fertile soil.

Settlement and agriculture have driven most of Bulgaria's wild animals out of the country's plains and valleys. Wildlife is now most commonly found in the rugged southwestern highlands, which support bears, wolves, elks, boars, foxes, and wildcats. Bulgaria's bird species include quails and turtledoves. Sturgeon, whitefish, and carp swim in Bulgaria's rivers, and a small seal colony lives on the Black Sea coast north of Varna.

in Sofia average 29° F. July, the warmest month in the capital, averages 70° F.

Milder temperatures are common on the Thracian Plain, where the Balkan Mountains shelter cities and farms from cold northern winds. Southerly breezes bring heavier precipitation to the area, which is humid in winter and hot and dry during the summer. Temperatures in Plovdiv, the largest town on the Thracian Plain, average 32° F in January and 75° F in July. The Black Sea coast and the southern portion of the Rhodope Mountains have warmer, sunnier climates.

Precipitation falls mostly as rain in the Bulgarian plains and lowlands and as snow in the highlands. A few mountain

Natural Resources

Bulgaria's most valuable natural resource is the black, fertile soil that is most abundant in the northern Danube Plateau. The Thracian Plain and the valley of the Maritsa River also boast good soils, although farms need irrigation in these areas to produce reliable harvests.

Coal is the country's most abundant energy source. Miners work deposits of lignite (brown coal) in several basins in the Balkan Mountains. Oil reserves are present at Tulenovo, near the Black Sea, and in offshore wells near Varna. Bulgaria, however, cannot supply its own energy needs and must import most of its oil and natural gas.

Metal ores have been important to Bulgaria's industrialization. Deposits of iron ore exist near Sofia and along the Black Sea near the port of Burgas. The Burgas Lowland also produces copper and manganese, an important ingredient in steel production. Bulgaria exports small quantities

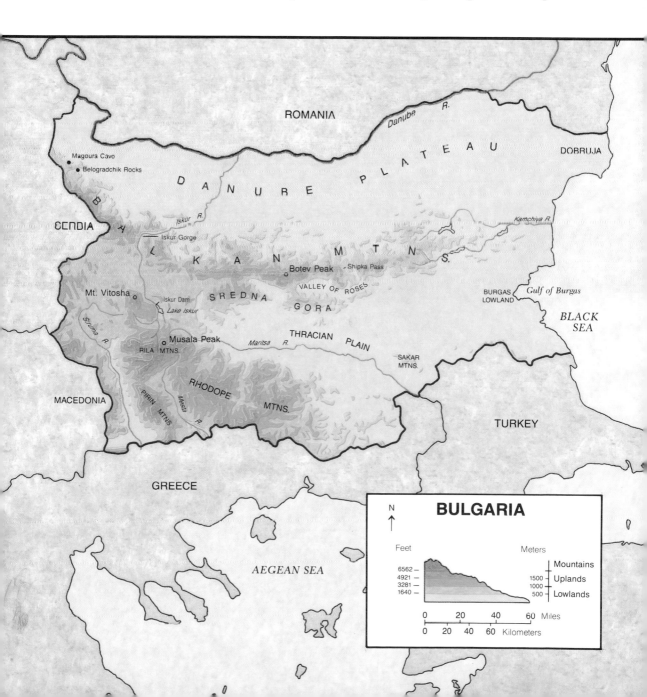

BULGARIA

N

Feet
6562
4921
3281
1640

Meters
1500 — Mountains
1000
500 — Uplands
— Lowlands

0   20   40   60 Miles
0 20 40 60 Kilometers

Government offices, museums, and department stores crowd the heart of Sofia, the capital of Bulgaria. To improve air quality in the city, developers built many factories and power plants far from the center.

Bulgarians, who love drama and music, often fill Sofia's theaters and concert halls to capacity. The Ivan Vazov National Theater, the country's largest, produces classical and modern plays by Bulgarian and foreign playwrights.

of the lead, zinc, and copper found in the Rhodope and Balkan mountains. Deposits of kaolin (a white clay used to make porcelain), pyrite, and sulfur also provide important raw materials.

Cities

Throughout much of their history, Bulgarians lived in remote and mountainous areas to escape Turkish rule. After parts of Bulgaria won independence in 1878, the population of the valleys and lowlands increased as farmers moved to more productive land. After World War II, the government established new industries in Bulgarian cities, and urban areas began to grow. By the early 1990s, when the population reached nine million, 68 percent of all Bulgarians lived in cities.

Sofia (population 1.1 million), Bulgaria's capital, lies in a high mountain basin in the western part of the country. An important transportation hub, Sofia links mountain passes that lead westward to Serbia, northward to the Danube Plateau, and eastward to the Thracian Plain. Sofia's factories produce textiles, chemicals, machinery, shoes, clothing, and transportation equipment.

The country's cultural capital as well as the seat of government, Sofia has universities, technical colleges, museums, and an opera house. An Islamic mosque (house of prayer) and a Jewish synagogue are open to worshipers, and many of the city's ancient Christian churches have been preserved and restored. The fountains, shade trees, and pleasant lawns of the Sofia City Garden offer a place to rest in the city's crowded center.

The ancient Thracians first settled the site of Sofia before 1000 B.C. The Romans captured the Thracian settlement in 29 B.C. and named it Serdica. Bulgars migrating into the Balkan region arrived in 809, and the city later came under the control of the Ottoman Empire. In the fourteenth century, the town took the name Sofia after the name of a local church. The capital of Bulgaria since 1879, Sofia suffered heavy bombing during World War II. Since the war, the city has been extensively rebuilt.

The country's second largest city, Plovdiv (population 350,000) is an important market town on the Maritsa River. Plovdiv traces its origins to the ancient Greeks, who built the city of Eumolpias on this site. Macedonians conquered Eumolpias in 341 B.C. The city later became the capital of the Roman province of Thrace.

Food-processing plants in Plovdiv package rice, fruit, tobacco, and wine. Other

In 1990 the Bulgarian National Assembly was the scene of a huge protest that led to a dramatic change in the nation's government.

Courtesy of Peace Corps/H. Dreyfuss

factories manufacture shoes, textiles, and metal goods. An important annual trade fair in Plovdiv has become a showcase for Bulgarian products. The city's tourist attractions include an ancient theater constructed entirely of fine marble. Not far from Plovdiv is an impressive fortress dating to the thirteenth century.

Varna (population 300,000), Bulgaria's principal Black Sea port, was also founded by the ancient Greeks, who called the city Odessus. Modern Varna has manufacturing facilities for textiles, furniture, ceramics, and diesel engines. A naval base and a naval school are also located in the city.

Burgas (population 145,000), to the south, faces the wide, deep Gulf of Burgas. Fish canneries, an oil refinery, and a huge chemical plant operate near the harbor. To attract tourists, the Bulgarian government has built several modern vacation resorts along the coast near Burgas.

Photo © Wynd Image

Traditional homes line the streets of an old neighborhood in Plovdiv. In many Bulgarian houses, wooden beams are used to extend and support the upper stories.

A painter from Thrace—an ancient kingdom that covered what is now Bulgaria—decorated this vase with a colorful scene of horses and their riders.

2) History and Government

The first inhabitants of the Balkan Peninsula were Stone Age hunters, who lived in the region as early as 250,000 years ago. Archaeologists have discovered prehistoric tools and weapons in several Bulgarian caves. Paintings of humans and animals in the Magoura Cave, near Vratsa in the Balkan Mountains, date to 3000 B.C.

At that time, a nomadic people known as the Thracians were settling in the valley of the Maritsa River and organizing the kingdom of Thrace. This state later came under the influence of the Greeks, who inhabited the cities, coastal lowlands, and islands of the Aegean Sea region. After 1000 B.C., Greek colonists also built several trading ports on the western coast of the Black Sea.

To strengthen their realm, the ancient Thracian kings allied with Athens, a powerful Greek city. But in the fourth century B.C., Thrace was attacked and defeated by Philip, the ruler of Macedonia in northern Greece. After Philip was assassinated in 336 B.C., his son Alexander the Great led Macedonian armies through Thrace and Asia Minor (modern Turkey) before conquering much of the Middle East and central Asia.

Roman Rule

Thrace regained its independence after the death of Alexander in 323 B.C. and the collapse of his empire. Yet the region's valuable gold mines soon attracted the

19

The Romans raised this gate in the walled city of Augusta (modern Hisarya), where modern visitors can see the remains of ancient marble baths. Since Thracian times, Hisarya has been famous for its healthy mineral springs.

Romans, who were expanding from their base on the Italian Peninsula. After defeating Macedonia in the second century B.C., the Romans drove northward to the Danube River. Rome established two provinces in the region—Moesia, between the Danube and the Balkan Mountains, and Thrace to the south.

Roman soldiers and farmers settled in these provinces and built new roads, for-

The Church of St. George was built in the fourth century A.D. during the reign of the Roman emperor Constantine. Like many historic Christian churches, St. George's stands directly over an older temple, where the people of Serdica (modern Sofia) once worshiped the pre-Christian Roman gods.

tifications, and cities. The valleys and plains of the region provided vital supplies of grain to Rome, which also recruited Thracian soldiers into its army. Moesia and Thrace remained peaceful until foreign invasions began to weaken the empire.

In the third century A.D., nomadic Goths from northern Europe attacked cities and farms on the Balkan Peninsula. The Huns of central and eastern Asia later invaded Moesia. In A.D. 330, the Roman emperor Constantine moved his capital to the Greek port of Byzantium (modern Istanbul), which he renamed Constantinople. This action led to the division of the empire into eastern and western halves.

The invasions from the north forced the Romans to abandon Thrace and Moesia in 395. In the fifth century, further attacks brought down the Western Roman Empire. The Eastern Roman Empire survived as the Byzantine Empire, which included the former Roman provinces in the Balkans. The Byzantine rulers followed the Christian religion, a Middle Eastern faith adopted by the emperor Constantine.

The Bulgarian Kingdom

In the sixth century, ethnic Slavs from the plains north of the Black Sea arrived in the Danube valley. Although the Byzantine Empire had built several fortresses in the area, the Slavs were strong enough to push southward into Moesia and Thrace. Ethnic Bulgars, who spoke a Turkic language and were led by khans (princes), invaded the region in the seventh century. The skilled Bulgar fighters defeated Byzantine forces that were sent to defend Moesia.

Eventually, the Bulgars intermarried with the Slavs and adopted the Slavic language. In 681 Khan Asparukh founded the first Bulgarian kingdom at his capital of Pliska in northeastern Bulgaria. Nobles ruled each of the realm's 10 provinces, while the boyars (landowners) formed a powerful and independent aristocracy. Landless peasants known as serfs worked

Photo by Dumbarton Oaks © 1993

Constantine made Christianity the Roman Empire's official religion and declared Constantinople (modern Istanbul, Turkey) to be his capital. After Constantine's death in A.D. 337, Bulgaria's history became closely tied with the Byzantine Empire, which spread the Eastern Orthodox faith to Bulgaria's Slavic and Bulgar settlers.

on the boyar estates. The serfs had few rights and were required to turn over a percentage of their crops to the boyars each year.

The kingdom came under frequent attack from the Byzantine Empire. Under Khan Krum, the Bulgarians defeated the Byzantine army in 811 and killed the emperor Nicephorus. Khan Krum followed his victory by claiming Byzantine territory and nearly overrunning Constantinople. His successors expanded the Bulgarian kingdom westward into Serbia and Macedonia and northward into what is now Romania.

In 863 Khan Boris I converted to the Christian faith and ordered his subjects

Photo by Anne-Marie Hupchick and Dennis P. Hupchick

The fortress at Belogradchik Rocks towered over the Danube River Valley, a route for many migrations and invasions on the Balkan Peninsula.

to become Christians. At the same time, Christian leaders were having bitter disagreements over church doctrine. As a result, Constantinople and Rome became rival religious centers. While these disputes continued, Boris asked the pope—the leader of the church in Rome—to appoint a Bulgarian archbishop. When the pope refused, Boris shifted his loyalty to Constantinople, and the Bulgarians adopted the Byzantine, or Orthodox, form of Christianity.

By the beginning of the tenth century, Bulgaria had become the most powerful realm on the Balkan Peninsula. The Slavic and Bulgar populations had merged to form a single nation of ethnic Bulgarians. Busy trade along the kingdom's rivers and roads enriched the monarchy and led Greek and Armenian merchants to settle in Bulgarian towns.

The Byzantine culture introduced by contact with Constantinople stimulated Bulgarian art, literature, and education. Clement, the disciple of a Byzantine missionary named Cyril, established the first Slavic literary school. About 900 Clement developed a written alphabet and named it Cyrillic after his former teacher.

Despite the kingdom's links to the Byzantine Empire, Simeon I, who became Bulgaria's ruler in 893, fell into a dispute with the Byzantine emperor. After defeating a Byzantine army, Simeon signed a treaty with the empire that awarded new territory in Macedonia and Thrace to Bulgaria. In 924 Bulgarian armies besieged Serbia and added it to the kingdom.

After Simeon's death in 927, Bulgaria began to weaken. Slavs from the Russian plains to the northeast invaded in 969 and captured the Bulgarian royal family. Seeing this as a threat to his own realm, the Byzantine emperor John I Tzimisces attacked and defeated the Slavs. Later, he annexed (took over) eastern Bulgaria.

Byzantine Conquest

The Byzantine emperor Basil II, known as the "Bulgar slayer," defeated the Bulgarian army in 1014. To prevent a counterattack, Basil ordered the blinding of 14,000 Bulgarian soldiers. He then conquered the remaining Bulgarian lands and brought them into the Byzantine Empire.

Under Byzantine rule, the Bulgarians suffered heavy taxes and economic decline. Several Bulgarian revolts failed, and the region suffered further destruction when Christian crusaders (religious warriors) marched through Bulgaria in the twelfth century.

Byzantine rule lasted until the 1180s, when the boyar brothers Asen and Peter staged a successful rebellion. The brothers founded the Second Bulgarian Empire with its capital at Veliko Turnovo in the Balkan Mountains. Weakened by their own internal rivalries, the Byzantine emperors later yielded Macedonia to this new Asenid dynasty (family of rulers).

In the early thirteenth century, Ivan Asen II added Albania and western Thrace to Bulgaria. Albania's location on the coast of the Adriatic Sea gave Bulgarian traders access to busy ports and to foreign markets for their goods. Bulgaria's growing wealth again attracted foreign merchants and immigrants. Trade increased rapidly, and the nation began minting its first coins.

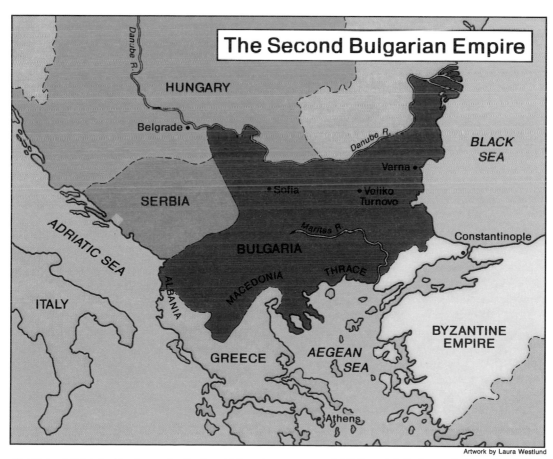

Artwork by Laura Westlund

The Second Bulgarian Empire, under the Asenid dynasty, was a powerful Balkan state that extended from the Adriatic Sea to the Black Sea. Although they ruled this empire for only 100 years, the Asenids greatly expanded the frontiers of their realm.

The battlements of Tsaravec, the oldest part of Veliko Turnovo, dominate the town's rocky heights. Here the rulers of the Second Bulgarian Empire protected their palaces with high towers and thick stone walls. The fall of Veliko Turnovo in 1393 to the invading Ottoman Turks brought about the swift end of the Bulgarian state.

Bulgaria's boyars and merchants were enjoying rising prosperity, but the serfs who worked on the kingdom's estates suffered poverty, hunger, and disease. Their harsh living conditions prompted Bulgaria's peasants to revolt in 1277. The uprising and a series of military defeats by Serbs and Hungarians weakened Bulgaria, which was forced to give up Macedonia and other important regions. In addition, a raid by Mongol warriors from Asia damaged cities, ports, and trading centers in northern Bulgaria.

As Bulgaria declined, a new and more serious threat was emerging. In the 1360s, Ottoman Turks from Asia Minor invaded the Balkan Peninsula and attacked Bulgarian towns in the Maritsa valley. The Bulgarian king Ivan Shishman III declared himself a vassal of the Turks, who had already overrun most of the Byzantine Empire. In 1393 Veliko Turnovo fell, and three years later the Ottoman Empire annexed Bulgaria.

Ottoman Rule

After conquering most of the eastern Mediterranean area, including all of the Balkan states, the Turks took control of Bulgaria's economy. Turkish farmers settled in the fertile valleys, driving most of the Bulgarians into the mountains. The Turkish sultan (ruler) levied heavy taxes on the boyars and on the townspeople who remained.

The Turks, who followed the Islamic faith, converted Christian churches to mosques. Some Bulgarians living under direct Turkish rule accepted Islam. These converts enjoyed exemption from taxes, and some of them gained important positions in the Turkish administration. Many of those who would not convert, however, were executed.

In 1453 the Turks conquered the city of Constantinople. The Byzantine Empire collapsed, and a long occupation of the Balkan Peninsula began. The Turkish beylerbey (governor) of the region made his headquarters in Sofia. From this cap-

The Ottoman Turks used a corps of loyal officers, known as Janissaries, to help them rule the Balkan Peninsula. The Turks educated and trained the Janissaries, many of whom were young Bulgarian slaves who had been forcibly converted to the religion of Islam.

ital, the Turks controlled provincial governors, who contributed money, food, and soldiers to the empire. The Turks seized more land from Bulgarian peasants and forced many of them to join the Turkish army.

The Bulgarians staged several revolts, but all of them failed. For centuries, the Bulgarian language and culture survived only in Orthodox Christian monasteries, where Bulgarians took refuge from Turkish rule. Throughout the fifteenth and sixteenth centuries, cities declined and farming estates fell into ruin. Turkish peasants claimed the abandoned agricultural land and turned their harvests over to the Turkish administration.

In order to more easily rule the region, the Turks tried to merge the Greek and Bulgarian populations in the seventeenth century. They allowed the Greek Orthodox

In 1453 the Ottoman Turks overwhelmed the defenders of Constantinople and captured the city, an event that brought down the Byzantine Empire. As a result, southeastern Europe was helpless to stop the conquests of the Turks, who ruled Bulgaria until the 1800s.

Church to take control of education in Bulgaria, and the Greek language temporarily replaced Bulgarian in the schools and churches. This campaign eventually failed, however, after a rebirth of Bulgarian culture occurred in the eighteenth century.

The Bulgarian Revival

By the late 1700s, a nationalist Bulgarian revival was under way. New schools, in which instructors used the Bulgarian language, taught history through ancient Bulgarian songs and folk ballads. Several historical works contributed to the growing sense of Bulgarian nationhood. Father Paisi, a Macedonian monk, authored *The Slav-Bulgarian History,* a book that inspired opposition to Turkish rule.

At the same time, the Russian Empire was expanding southward into the Balkan Peninsula. The Russians sought control of ports and trade in the Black Sea region, which linked the vast plains of Russia to the Aegean and Mediterranean seas. The Russian czar (emperor), who led an Orthodox nation, pressed the Turks to allow the Bulgarians greater religious and political liberty.

The expense of maintaining their huge realm weakened the Turks, who were facing revolts in Greece, Romania, and other occupied lands. The independence fighter Georgi Rakovsky, who organized guerrilla bands in Serbia and Romania, trained a volunteer force to sweep across the Balkan Mountains and ignite a revolt. Vasil Levski worked in Bulgarian villages to build an underground network of revolutionaries.

Farmers and townspeople mingle at a busy street market in Sofia. The Turks converted a nearby Orthodox church into a mosque (Islamic house of prayer).

Carrying rifles and whips, Turkish guards force Bulgarian prisoners to work on Turkish fortifications during Bulgaria's war of liberation in the 1870s.

At first, the Bulgarians met with failure. Rakovsky died in 1867, and Levski was captured and executed in 1873. Three years later, the Turks put down the Bulgarian uprising with great cruelty. The Bulgarians then turned to Russia for help. In 1877 the czar declared war on the Ottoman Empire and ordered an invasion of the Balkans. Bulgarian and Russian volunteers defeated the Turkish forces in a series of fierce battles.

In 1878 the Turks agreed to the Treaty of San Stefano, which stripped Turkey of its European territories and added Thrace and Macedonia to Bulgaria. But many European nations feared that the fall of the Ottoman realm would lead to Russian domination of the Balkans. At the Congress of Berlin three months later, the European powers forced the return of Macedonia and Thrace to Turkey. Northern Bulgaria gained its freedom, while the eastern part of the country became Eastern Rumelia, a semi-independent territory under Turkish control.

Independence

In 1879 Bulgarian leaders met at Veliko Turnovo and adopted a constitution. The document established the National

Vasil Levski, the revolutionary hero of the Bulgarians, attended military school in neighboring Serbia before leading the drive for Bulgarian independence.

In the late nineteenth century, the gradual withdrawal of Turkey from the Balkans led to conflict among the newly independent nations of the region. In 1885 Serbia attacked Bulgaria with the hope of gaining territory. Within five months, however, Bulgaria defeated the Serbians. Territorial conflicts would continue in the Balkans during the twentieth century.

Assembly, a unicameral (one-house) parliament whose representatives would be elected by a vote of all Bulgarian citizens. The Bulgarian assembly later chose Alexander of Battenberg, a German prince and a nephew of the Russian czar, to become the Bulgarian ruler.

Alexander made many unpopular changes in the government, however, and also suspended the constitution. For several years, the prince ruled the country with the help of Russian military officers. Bulgaria suffered bitter disputes between Liberals, who supported the constitution, and Conservatives, who supported Alexander. Seeking to resolve the crisis, Alexander restored the constitution in 1883.

Two years later, the people of Eastern Rumelia revolted against the Turks and joined their region to Bulgaria. Alarmed at the growing power of Bulgaria, Russia supported a conspiracy to kidnap Alexander and to establish a new regime. Although the conspiracy was stopped by Stefan Stambolov, the president of the National Assembly, Alexander abdicated (gave up) the throne in 1886.

The assembly then elected another German, Prince Ferdinand, to rule the country. A capable and energetic leader, Ferdinand united the nation's political factions. In 1908 Ferdinand took advantage of the Turks' weakness and declared all of Bulgaria, including Eastern Rumelia, to be independent.

Under Ferdinand's government, Bulgaria began to modernize its industry and agriculture. Education was expanded, and literacy greatly increased. Nevertheless, difficult working conditions for factory laborers led to the founding of the Social Democratic party, which fought for the interests of workers. An Agrarian Union party represented Bulgaria's peasants.

War and Defeat

Despite their hard-won independence, Bulgarians were dissatisfied with the division of territory in the Balkan region. Thrace and Macedonia, which were still under Turkish control, contained large Bulgarian populations. Bulgaria's leaders sought to bring all ethnic Bulgarians into a single nation. In addition, to improve their trade and economy, the Bulgarians wanted control of a port on the Aegean Sea.

In 1912 Serbia, Bulgaria, and Greece formed an alliance and declared war on Turkey. This First Balkan War resulted in a victory for Bulgaria and its allies in 1913. But these nations could not agree on a division of territory. Serbia, Greece, and Bulgaria all laid claim to Macedonia, leading to another conflict in which Bulgaria stood alone against its Balkan neighbors. Bulgaria was quickly defeated in the Second Balkan War. The treaty that settled this war in 1913 returned some Bulgarian land to Turkey and awarded only a small portion of Macedonia to the Bulgarians.

By this time, rivalry over trade and territory had led Europe's nations to form two grand alliances. Austria-Hungary, Germany, and Turkey (the Central Powers) joined forces to balance the power of Russia, Britain, Italy, and France (the Allies). Meanwhile, several Balkan peoples were seeking freedom from Austria-Hungary. In the summer of 1914, a Serbian assassinated a member of the Austrian royal family. Austria-Hungary then declared war against Serbia, an ally of Russia. This conflict quickly drew the Allies and the Central Powers into World War I.

Bulgaria saw the war as an opportunity to reclaim the territory lost during the Balkan conflicts. The Bulgarian government sided with the Central Powers, signing a treaty with Germany in 1915 that promised the return of Macedonia. Fighting broke out in the same year along Bulgaria's borders with Serbia and Romania.

The war soon caused violent unrest within Bulgaria, where politicians strongly disagreed on the country's policies. The Social Democratic and Agrarian Union parties, for example, openly criticized Bulgaria's involvement in the war.

In the fall of 1918, the Central Powers surrendered to the Allies, who forced Bulgaria to sign a treaty that transferred parts of Thrace and Macedonia to Greece. In addition, Bulgarian territory was claimed by the new Kingdom of the Serbs, Croats, and Slovenes (later Yugoslavia),

Courtesy of Stephane Groueff

Under Ferdinand, who was elected by the Bulgarians as their prince in 1887, the nation began to modernize its industries, agriculture, and educational system.

which included Serbia. Angry at the defeat, the Bulgarian army threatened to revolt and seize power. To maintain the monarchy, Ferdinand abdicated in favor of his son Boris III.

Postwar Turmoil

The end of the war brought chaos to Bulgaria, where unemployment was rising and many rural families were suffering famine. In the cities, poor and hungry factory laborers joined massive strikes that brought manufacturing to a standstill.

In 1919 Alexander Stamboliyski, a leader of the Agrarian Union party, became the country's prime minister. Stamboliyski's strongest support came from the country's peasants, who still made up 80 percent of the population. His administration improved education and reformed Bulgaria's legal codes and tax system. The government built new roads to improve trade and transportation, and Stamboliyski arranged for the transfer of some land to peasant ownership.

Divisions among the country's political groups continued, however. A faction of the Social Democratic party organized a Bulgarian Communist party. Russian Communists had overthrown their government and, in 1922, established the Union of Soviet Socialist Republics. Fearing a similar overthrow in Bulgaria, many Bulgarian politicians and military officers turned against the Bulgarian Communists.

During the 1920s, the country suffered economic decline as prices rose and strikes continued to paralyze the cities. Militants seeking self-rule for Macedonia carried out

Artwork by Laura Westlund

Bulgaria adopted its flag in 1878, when the Treaty of San Stefano officially established an independent Bulgarian state. The color white represents peace, while red and green stand for courage and for abundant harvests, respectively.

In July 1923, revolutionary troops guarded a flag bearer who sided with Alexander Stamboliyski, Bulgaria's defeated prime minister. After taking their prisoner, the guards cut Stamboliyski's personal emblem from the flag.

terrorist attacks, and Communists and Conservatives battled in the streets of Sofia. Stamboliyski remained unpopular in the cities and in the armed forces. In 1923 a group of Conservative politicians and army officers formed the Military League, a secret organization that overthrew and assassinated the prime minister.

After Stamboliyski's death, a civil war broke out between Bulgaria's political factions. The Conservatives, who were allied with the military, eventually prevailed. The new government arrested and tried many of its opponents and outlawed the Communist party. During the late 1920s and early 1930s, Bulgaria endured continuing terrorism and harsh rule by the country's army officers.

Another crisis erupted in 1934 when a coalition of reform parties suspended the constitution. Kimon Georgiev, a leader of the Military League, became the new prime minister. Georgiev banned all political parties and dissolved the legislature. These actions lessened support for Georgiev, however. In 1935 King Boris forced him out of office and imposed a royal dictatorship on Bulgaria.

World War II

During the 1930s, new regimes were also taking power in Italy and Germany. Under Adolf Hitler, the leader of the Nazi party, Germany denounced the treaties that ended World War I and began to rearm. Trade between Bulgaria and Germany brought the two countries closer together. Boris also formed ties with Italy by marrying the daughter of the Italian king.

When Hitler ordered the invasion of Poland in the summer of 1939, the Allied

During World War II (1939–1945), a German artillery unit crosses a muddy stream while advancing through Bulgarian territory. The Bulgarian government allied with Germany at the outbreak of the war and allowed German forces to pass through the country on the way to attacking Greece.

nations of Britain and France immediately declared war on Germany. World War II quickly drew in the Balkan nations, which were still disputing their territory and boundaries. In 1940 Germany forced Romania to surrender part of Dobruja, a region along the Black Sea coast, to Bulgaria.

In the next year, as Germany attacked Greece and Yugoslavia, Bulgaria occupied land in Serbia, Thrace, and Macedonia. The Bulgarian government allied with Hitler and declared war on the Allies in December 1941. Despite their ties to Germany, the Bulgarians—who remembered Russia's help in the fight for Bulgarian

Georgi Dimitrov, a founder of the Bulgarian Communist party, headed Bulgaria's underground resistance to German occupation during World War II. After the war, he became Bulgaria's first Communist prime minister.

independence—refused to join a German attack on the Soviet Union in the summer of 1942.

Bulgaria escaped much of the war's destruction until 1943, when Allied air forces bombed Sofia and other cities. As German forces retreated in September 1944, Bulgaria sought peace with the Allies. At the same time, however, Soviet forces driving into the Balkan Peninsula occupied the country.

The Soviets arrested Bulgarian officials and allowed the Fatherland Front, a coalition of Communists and other parties, to seize power. By the end of the war in May 1945, Bulgaria had lost most of the territory it had won while allied with Germany.

Courtesy of James Marrinan

A modern Bulgarian stamp commemorates the young king Simeon II, who succeeded his father, Otto, during World War II. After the war, the Bulgarian Communists took power, ousted Simeon, and brought down the Bulgarian monarchy.

Artwork by Laura Westlund

Although Bulgaria allied with Germany during the war, the Bulgarian government refused to join a German invasion of the Soviet Union, a Communist nation that lay east of Bulgaria. In 1945, as the Germans retreated into central Europe, Soviet forces marched into the Balkans and installed a Communist government in Bulgaria.

Courtesy of Ivan Grigorov

In the 1970s, Todor Zhivkov, the leader of the Bulgarian Communist party, spoke to a rally under a gigantic poster of Soviet leader Leonid Brezhnev. Brezhnev's huge public images earned him the nickname "Big Brother" in Bulgaria, a nation that maintained close ties to the Soviet Union until the overthrow of Zhivkov in 1989.

Communist Rule

In the years following the war, the Soviet Union dominated Bulgaria's affairs. Communist party members took control of the Fatherland Front and eliminated many of their opponents. In 1946 Bulgaria held a plebiscite (popular vote) that abolished the monarchy and established a republic. The Fatherland Front won a large majority in the legislature. Georgi Dimitrov, a leader of the Bulgarian Communists, became the country's prime minister.

Under Dimitrov's direction, the government wrote a new constitution modeled on that of the Soviet Union. Power was placed in the hands of the Communist party first secretary (leader). A few small committees, whose members belonged to the party, set policy and issued directives to industry and to the armed forces. The National Assembly automatically passed laws written by a State Council.

The government placed factories under centralized control and began to organize private farms into collectives, on which rural laborers became state employees. The Communist party banned opposing political parties, took control of the media, and brought the Bulgarian Orthodox Church and all other religious groups under state supervision.

In 1950 Vulko Chervenkov became first secretary of the Bulgarian Communist party. Under Chervenkov's regime, Bulgarian industry and trade were tied directly to the economy of the Soviet Union. As a member of the Soviet bloc, Bulgaria ended its trade with the nations of western Europe.

Nevertheless, Chervenkov lost favor with the Soviet government in 1954, when a new Soviet leader, Nikita Khrushchev, came to power. In that year, Chervenkov resigned his post as first secretary and was replaced by Todor Zhivkov. In 1962 Zhivkov ousted several of his rivals from the Communist party and named himself chairman of the State Council. Despite an attempt to overthrow him in April 1965, Zhivkov remained in power throughout the 1970s and 1980s.

Bulgaria's economy stagnated under Zhivkov's rule. The system of central planning led to inefficiency in the production and distribution of goods. Bulgaria exported many of its products at low prices to the Soviet Union and to other Communist nations. Within Bulgaria, food, consumer goods, and housing became increasingly scarce, and many Bulgarians suffered a declining standard of living.

Recent Events

During the 1980s, the chronic shortages put pressure on Zhivkov to reform Bulgaria's economic and political systems. Fearing a loss of Soviet support, however, Zhivkov resisted new policies and forced several reformers out of their government posts. These actions turned pro-reform members of the Bulgarian Communist party against their leader.

The Communist nations of Europe underwent a great upheaval in 1989. In Bulgaria and other countries, discontented citizens demonstrated in the streets and formed underground political parties. Weakened by its own internal problems, the Soviet Union could do little to prevent the downfall of Communist governments in the Balkans. In November 1989, Petar Mladenov, Bulgaria's foreign minister, gained the support of several powerful government officials and forced Zhivkov to resign.

At the same time, opposition groups were forming the Union of Democratic Forces (UDF), a coalition of non-Communist parties. Early in 1990, the National Assembly legalized Bulgaria's new parties. The Communists tried to shed their unpopular image by renaming their organization the Socialist party. In April 1990, the

Courtesy of Ivan Grigorov

Two women leave a crowded grocery store during the winter of 1991. Although Communist rule had recently ended, Bulgaria's economic reforms were slow to ease the severe shortages of food and consumer goods.

assembly elected Mladenov to the new post of president.

In June, after 45 years of Communist rule, Bulgaria held its first open parliamentary elections. The Socialist party won a majority in the assembly, but the UDF gained enough seats to form a strong opposing bloc. After the UDF supported a massive strike among Sofia's university students, Mladenov resigned. The assembly then elected Zhelyu Zhelev, the leader of the UDF, as the new president. Zhelev became Bulgaria's first non-Communist head of state since World War II. In December 1992, Ljuben Berov became Bulgaria's prime minister.

Bulgaria's new government is lessening central control of the economy. The government is also planning to sell state-owned industries in a process known as privatization. Although shortages have eased, prices are high for many essential goods. In addition, the privatization of industries is causing rising unemployment. Although they support the new political system, many Bulgarians are struggling to survive in the country's weak economy.

Government

The fall of Bulgaria's Communist regime caused a transformation of the nation's government. In 1990 Bulgaria's revised constitution allowed opposition parties to participate in all branches of government. Bulgaria now has a unicameral parliament, the Grand National Assembly. Its 240 deputies are elected to five-year terms by a popular vote of adults in their districts.

The assembly elects the Bulgarian president, who serves as the head of state and as commander in chief. The Council of Ministers consists of 15 ministers of various departments as well as a prime minister and three deputies. As the head of the council, the prime minister acts as the executive leader of the government.

Bulgaria is divided into seven *oblasti* (provinces) and the city of Sofia, which has the status of a separate *oblast.* More than 1,100 urban communities have been designated *obshtini.* Some obshtini are made up of several rural villages. Elected executive councils administer the oblasti and obshtini.

The Supreme Court, whose judges are elected to five-year terms, is the nation's highest judicial body. A system of provincial courts operates within Bulgaria's oblasti, and 103 local courts decide lesser crimes. A chief prosecutor is responsible for overseeing the legal system and for resolving important disputes.

Filip Dimitrov, who served as the first post-Communist prime minister of Bulgaria, led the government during the political reforms of 1991 and 1992.

Skaters and guards pose together in downtown Sofia. Bulgarians once feared arrest by the local police for expressing anti-Communist political views in public.

3) The People

The many centuries of Ottoman rule had a lasting effect on Bulgaria's people. During this period, most Bulgarians lived outside the cities and supported themselves by farming. After the Turkish withdrawal in 1878, most of Bulgaria's people remained in the countryside. Bulgarian peasants formed extended families, in which daughters moved but sons remained within the household after marriage.

Bulgarian society underwent rapid changes after the Communist government was established in 1945. The regime encouraged rural families to move to the cities, where new industrial jobs were available. Traditional extended families scattered to distant towns and cities. An urban class of clerks and government officials formed, and many Bulgarians distanced themselves from their roots in the countryside. In addition, women entered the labor force for the first time. By the early 1990s, women made up almost half of Bulgaria's industrial workers.

A woman offers produce for sale in an open-air market.

About 70 percent of Bulgaria's nine million people now live in urban areas, which have grown steadily since World War II. Nevertheless, the country's population density—210 people per square mile—is one of the lowest in Europe. The Sofia area, the Thracian Plain, and the Black Sea coast are the most heavily populated regions, while the rugged mountains of the southwest and the Balkan range support fewer people.

A shepherd and his flock pass through a rural village. Bulgaria remained a largely agricultural country well into the twentieth century, and a high percentage of Bulgarians still farm the land.

Photo by Anne-Marie Hupchick and Dennis P. Hupchick

A wedding party travels through Nesebur, a town on Bulgaria's Black Sea coast. Despite the Communist regime's restrictions on religion, Orthodox ceremonies survived among Bulgaria's Christians.

Although Bulgaria's population grew rapidly during the early twentieth century, the birthrate slowed to 11 per 1,000 in the early 1990s. At the same time, the death rate stood at 12 per 1,000 people. As a result, Bulgaria's population stopped growing and began to decline.

Ethnic Groups

Eighty-five percent of Bulgaria's people are ethnic Bulgarians, who are descended from the Slavs and Bulgars who arrived in the sixth and seventh centuries. Ethnic Bulgarians also live in Greece, Romania, Serbia, Macedonia, and Ukraine.

Although many ethnic Turks emigrated after Bulgaria's independence, they still make up about 8 percent of the population. The Turks live as farmers in eastern Bulgaria, in the Rhodope Mountains, and in the valley of the Danube River. During the 1980s, Bulgaria's leaders banned the use of the Turkish language and forced ethnic Turks to take Bulgarian names. The government struck down these measures in December 1989.

Bulgaria is also home to ethnic Greeks, Armenians, and Russians. These groups arrived before and during the Turkish occupation to work as merchants and traders in Bulgaria's cities and ports. Nomadic Gypsies, who make up about 2 percent of the population, still roam the Bulgarian countryside. Many historians believe that Gypsies migrated to eastern Europe from northern India many centuries ago. Modern Gypsies speak the Romany language, in addition to Bulgarian, and work as metalsmiths, horse traders, and musicians.

Health and Education

Under the Communist government, Bulgarians benefited from extended social services. The government built new hospitals

Strollers walk past a small park in Melnik. Once a bustling trading center with a population of 14,000, Melnik suffered heavy damage during the Balkan Wars. The town now is home to about 400 people.

and created a network of public clinics. Health care was free, and the state provided sickness benefits, disability pay, and retirement pensions. Bulgaria's health system suffered from inefficiency, however. Many patients had to wait for long periods to receive care from underpaid and poorly trained doctors.

With the fall of Communism, Bulgaria's social security system is now undergoing important changes. To save money, the government may cut back or eliminate some social benefits and health programs. In addition, many doctors have established private practices and now charge patients directly for medical services.

Improved health care after World War II brought many infectious diseases under control. As a result, life expectancy for Bulgarians increased to 71 years, an

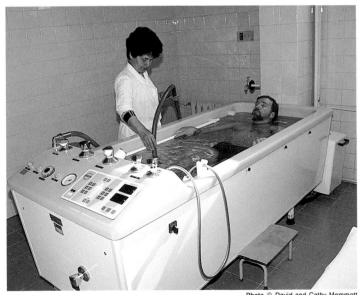

A nurse attends a patient in Hisarya. Many people visit this town for its mineral waters, and the local spas offer more than 40 different treatments for a wide variety of ailments.

average figure for eastern European countries. Infant mortality, the number of babies that die within the first year of birth, stands at 17 per 1,000, which is also average for the region.

The Bulgarian school system also expanded rapidly after World War II. The Communist party based its reforms on the Soviet model, in which education became the means to inspire loyalty to the party's leaders and policies. Schools also emphasized technical training for the many new workers who were entering the country's industrial workforce.

Students must attend school between the ages of 7 and 16. Important subjects include history, sciences, mathematics, grammar, and languages. After completing this primary school, students must pass a final examination to continue their education. Most young people then follow courses in scientific, vocational, or technical training. Bulgaria has 25 institutions of higher learning, including the University of Sofia. In addition, many schools offer night courses for adults.

Religion

Bulgarians have been Christians since Khan Boris I converted to this faith in the ninth century. The majority of ethnic

Students at this technical school in Varna specialize in economics.

Courtesy of Ivan Grigorov

Worshipers and Orthodox church leaders attend an outdoor ceremony during the winter of 1991.

Photo by Anne-Marie Hupchick and Dennis P. Hupchick

Bulgarians belong to the Bulgarian Orthodox Church, an independent branch of Eastern Orthodox Christianity. Bulgaria's Armenians, Russians, and Greeks also have their own Orthodox churches.

During the eighteenth and nineteenth centuries, the Bulgarian church led the drive for independence from the Turks. After World War II, however, the Bulgarian Communist party discouraged religious schooling. Nevertheless, families continued to instruct their children in the faith, and the church remained an important part of everyday life. Orthodox priests still conduct most baptisms, wed-

A resident of the St. Nikola Monastery holds the key to this seventeenth-century religious complex.

dings, and funerals. After the fall of the Communist regime, Bulgaria's government lifted all restrictions on religious practice.

Bulgaria's ethnic Turks follow the Islamic religion, which arrived with the Ottoman armies in the fourteenth and fifteenth centuries. A mufti leads Islamic believers in Bulgaria, where a few mosques remain open to worshipers. There are also a small number of ethnic Bulgarians, known as Pomaks, who are Muslims (followers of Islam). The Pomaks converted to Islam during the Turkish occupation.

Before World War II, Bulgaria's Jews made up a mostly urban community of 50,000 members. Although most Bulgarian Jews survived the war, Jewish emigration to the Middle East was heavy under Bulgaria's postwar regime. Bulgarian Jews, many of whom live in Sofia, now number less than 10,000.

Language and Literature

The Bulgarian language is an ancient Slavic tongue that is related to Russian. As the medieval Bulgarian kingdom grew, Bulgarian became the first Slavic literary language and was used in religious writings throughout the Slavic world. The Bulgarians have adapted words from

Dating to 1493, this page contains the first printing of the Cyrillic alphabet. Named for Saint Cyril, an Orthodox missionary, Cyrillic became the alphabet of Bulgarian and of other Slavic languages.

A road sign carries the names of its Bulgarian destinations in Cyrillic and Roman lettering.

Old Church Slavonic, from Russian, from Greek, and from Turkish. Under the country's Communist government, instruction in Russian—the official language of the Soviet Union—was compulsory in Bulgarian schools. The new government dropped this requirement in the early 1990s.

Distinct dialects of Bulgarian exist in various regions of the country, but most Bulgarians can easily understand one another. Many ethnic Bulgarians speak a second language, the most common being Russian or English. The Cyrillic alphabet, which is named after the missionary Saint Cyril, is used to write Russian, Bulgarian, and several other Slavic languages.

Although all of Bulgaria's people speak Bulgarian, other ethnic groups also have distinct languages. Turks still use the Turkish language, which survived the government ban of the 1980s. Greeks, Gypsies, and Armenians speak their own languages in addition to Bulgarian.

Bulgarian literature has its roots in the works of Saint Cyril and Saint Methodius, who translated the Greek New Testament for use by the Slavic people of the Balkans. Religious literature flourished until the time of the Ottoman conquest in the fifteenth century. Under Ottoman rule, folk tales and ballads survived to carry on the nation's literary tradition.

By the late 1700s, writers such as Father Paisi were reviving Bulgarian nationalism through their historical and religious works. Paisi's *The Slav-Bulgarian History*, written in 1762, was the first of many books that appeared in the early nineteenth century, when Bulgarians established their first modern schools and printing shops.

Father Paisi, an eighteenth-century monk, sparked a revival of Bulgarian nationalism with his writings on Bulgaria's culture and history.

44

The writers Khristo Botev and Ivan Vazov fanned the flames of revolution against Turkey in the late 1800s. Vazov's novel *Under the Yoke,* which gained an international audience, described the harsh conditions endured by Bulgarians living under Ottoman rule. Vazov's writing has remained a strong influence on modern Bulgarian literature.

Twentieth-century writers, including Yordan Yovkov and Elin Pelin, turned to Bulgaria's rural society for inspiration in their novels and short stories. Dimiter Dimov's book *Tobacco* described revolutionary tobacco workers before and during World War II. Under Communist rule, the government placed tight restrictions on the style and subject matter of published works. The Communist party closely supervised writers' unions and controlled the publication of books, newspapers, and magazines.

Although the state supported many Bulgarian writers, most resisted the restrictions placed on them. In the early 1990s, small, private publishing houses were operating, as were journals and newspapers that freely expressed a wide range of public opinion.

Art and Music

The earliest Bulgarian artists worked exclusively with religious themes and subjects. The powerful Byzantine Empire greatly influenced the kingdom's painters, who began to combine Byzantine and Slavic artistic styles during the 800s.

Bulgarian artists created frescoes (paintings finished on wet plaster) and icons

A Sofia bookseller offers pamphlets and books in support of the Union of Democratic Forces, Bulgaria's non-Communist governing coalition.

Chandeliers and paintings of Christian saints decorate the interior of the Alexander Nevsky cathedral in Sofia.

(religious paintings on wood) in Orthodox monasteries, where masters of wood carving and icon painting offered instruction in their crafts. Some Bulgarian painters specialized in creating religious miniatures, small yet detailed works that could be carried by the faithful.

Bulgarian art stagnated until the nineteenth century, when the fight for independence gave rise to the National Revival movement in the arts. Zahari Zograf, a leading National Revival painter, decorated churches and monasteries throughout the country with his striking frescoes. Many early twentieth-century painters drew inspiration from rural life.

After World War II, the new Bulgarian regime adopted the doctrine of socialist realism for artists, writers, filmmakers, and composers. Strict guidelines required artists to glorify the social and economic achievements of Communism. Sculpture in this style still decorates public squares and buildings throughout Bulgaria. Nikolai Masterov, a noted modern painter, resisted socialist realism and instead used abstract shapes and designs.

Bulgaria's tradition of folk handicrafts includes carpet weaving and embroidery. Woodworkers and masons lavishly decorated many of the houses of wealthy Bulgarians in a distinctive, ornate style.

The Bulgarian opera star Nikolai Ghiaurov sings the role of Boris Gudonov. Bulgarians enjoy all forms of vocal music, including folk songs, choral music, and classical opera.

Folk songs and ballads kept Bulgarian music alive during the Turkish occupation. Flutes, bagpipes, and simple stringed instruments accompany folk songs and the *horo*, a circle dance. Modern Bulgarians love choral singing as well as opera, and the country supports five opera theaters.

Boris Christoff, Nikolai Ghiaurov, and Elena Nikolai became world-famous opera singers. Recordings of the Bulgarian State Female Vocal Choir, which performs traditional songs, are international bestsellers. Sofia, Burgas, and Varna host annual music festivals.

The Bulgarian State Female Vocal Choir performs traditional Bulgarian folk music for a worldwide audience. The group's two recordings have been bestsellers in many European countries.

Workers at a Bulgarian farming co-operative, in which members share both work and profits, gather to enjoy the fruits of their labors.

Food

Bulgarians enjoy a hearty traditional cuisine that draws on a wide variety of meats, fruits, and vegetables. Lamb, veal, and pork are central to many Bulgarian dishes, including *kebapchetas* (grilled meat patties spiced with black pepper, onions, and paprika). *Kavarma* is a hot stew containing pork, mushrooms, and vegetables. Meat, onions, herbs, mushrooms, and tomatoes are skewered and roasted to make *shishkebap*. Cooks stuff eggplant with onions, carrots, celery, and tomatoes to prepare cold *imama bajalda*. *Sirene gjuveche* is a dish made with butter, paprika, tomatoes, and goat cheese. Main courses are

Shoppers inspect fresh produce at an outdoor market in Sofia.

often accompanied by Bulgaria's abundant produce, including potatoes, eggplant, tomatoes, onions, and carrots.

Bulgarians begin many of their meals with thick soups. Monastery soup contains beans and vegetables. Cucumber, walnuts, yogurt, and dill are the ingredients in cold *tarator* soup. Cooks make *pitka*, a favorite Bulgarian bread, with yogurt, eggs, and cheese.

Bulgaria's thick yogurts are popular all over the world. Known as *kiselo mliako*, Bulgarian yogurt is made from the milk of sheep, goats, or cows. Bulgarians also enjoy a wide variety of fresh fruits, including cherries, strawberries, apricots, raspberries, apples, pears, melons, plums, and grapes.

Banitza, a sweet, cheese-filled pastry, is often eaten with yogurt for dessert. Baklava and *lokum* are traditional Turkish sweets. Bulgarians enjoy fruit juices, lemonade, tea, and thick, strong coffee. Adults often sample *rakiya* (plum or grape brandy) before meals. Bulgaria also produces red and white wines, as well as a liqueur made from rose petals.

Sports and Recreation

Soccer, Bulgaria's favorite team sport, is played by amateur squads and a national professional team. All the major cities have their own soccer teams, and young and old Bulgarians follow league play with great interest. Basketball, another popular team sport, is played among amateur clubs. Each year the country's best cyclists compete in the Tour of Bulgaria.

Under Communist rule, Bulgaria trained many champion weight lifters and wrestlers. Norair Novrikian was a two-time Olympic champion in weight lifting. Sevdalin Marinov achieved a weight lifting record during the 1988 Olympics. Stefka Kostadinova is a world champion high jumper.

Most Bulgarians participate in recreational sports. Many city dwellers enjoy hiking in the country's wild and mountainous areas. Mountain climbing is popular in the Rhodope Mountains. The Black Sea coast offers waterskiing, sailing, and windsurfing. Several of the country's lakes have recreational facilities. New winter sports resorts attract skiers to the Rila Mountains and to the highlands near Sofia.

Weight lifter Yordan Bikov jumps for joy after winning a gold medal for Bulgaria during the 1972 Summer Olympics. Bulgaria has a long tradition of victories in Olympic weight lifting and wrestling.

Courtesy of International Olympic Committee

49

A diesel train carries industrial freight through the Bulgarian countryside. Railroads have long been the most important means of cargo and passenger transport in Bulgaria.

4) The Economy

Agriculture dominated Bulgaria's economy until the late 1940s, when the new Communist regime began a rapid industrialization. The government seized private businesses and made Bulgarian workers employees of the state. Administrators set production goals, wages, and prices, and Bulgaria ended most of its trade with western Europe.

Bulgaria joined a Communist bloc of nations in eastern Europe, in which trade was closely linked to the economy of the Soviet Union. The Bulgarian government closely followed the Soviet Union's lead in establishing production goals. Instead of making industrial goods for domestic use, Bulgarian laborers processed raw materials and machine parts for final assembly in Soviet factories.

The rapid development gradually raised the standard of living in Bulgarian cities, which attracted many new workers from farms in the countryside. But the system of central planning also led to inefficiency. Shortages occurred as government officials were unable to coordinate production

Bulgaria's new government has transferred several state-operated farming cooperatives to private owners—a step called privatization. This farmer now tends livestock that he can sell for a profit.

to meet demand. Bulgaria also borrowed money from foreign nations to help its development. By the 1970s, these heavy debts were slowing production and new investment. The government adopted several reforms, yet the economy stagnated in the late 1980s.

In the early 1990s, Bulgaria's new government planned to create an open, market economy by selling state-owned industries and farms. This difficult process, which allows money-losing businesses to close, is causing severe unemployment.

Courtesy of Kenneth Egertson

Courtesy of Kenneth Egertson

After World War II, the migration of rural families to the cities of Bulgaria resulted in a construction boom. Nevertheless, housing was in short supply, and many families had to wait a long time before moving into government-built apartments.

51

Sacks of rose petals await processing in a Plovdiv plant. About 250 pounds of rose petals are needed to distill a single ounce of attar of roses.

In addition, the $11 billion foreign debt makes it difficult for Bulgaria to buy imported goods or to upgrade its factories. The fall of Communist regimes in eastern Europe and the economic decline in the region have hurt Bulgaria's export markets.

As a result, many companies are cutting production or going bankrupt.

Manufacturing

Bulgaria had only textile mills and a few other light industries before the Communist takeover of the late 1940s. With investment and materials supplied by the Soviet Union, the new regime greatly expanded heavy industry, including the production of building materials, chemicals, fuels, machinery, and finished metals. By the 1960s, manufacturing made up the largest sector of the Bulgarian economy and currently produces nearly three-quarters of all the nation's goods.

A huge petrochemical complex at Burgas makes a variety of industrial chemicals as well as essential fuels.

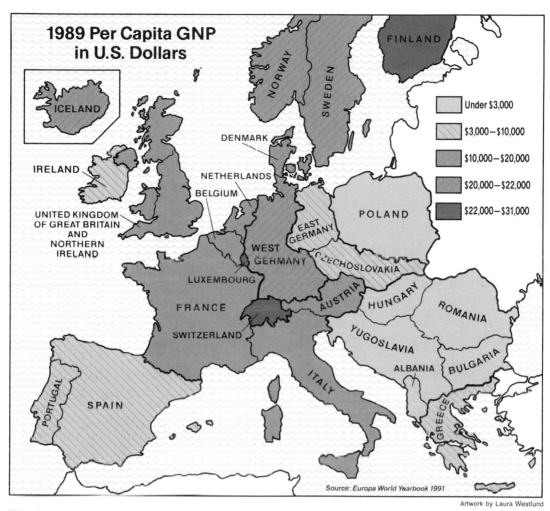

1989 Per Capita GNP in U.S. Dollars

Legend:
- Under $3,000
- $3,000–$10,000
- $10,000–$20,000
- $20,000–$22,000
- $22,000–$31,000

Source: *Europa World Yearbook 1991*

Artwork by Laura Westlund

This chart compares the average productivity per person—calculated by gross national product (GNP) per capita—for 26 European countries. The GNP is the value of all goods and services produced by a country in a year. To arrive at the GNP per capita, each nation's total GNP is divided by its population. The resulting dollar amounts are one measure of the standard of living in each country. Bulgaria's 1989 figure of $2,320 was one of the lowest in Europe, reflecting a stagnant economy that grew increasingly inefficient in the final years of Communist rule.

Iron and steel plants operate in Kremikovtsi and in Pernik, and chemical works exist near Plovdiv. Industries in the ports of Varna, Burgas, and Ruse benefit from their transportation links to eastern European markets. Bulgarian enterprises also produce glass, porcelain, clothing, and furniture, as well as tractors, ships, computers, and appliances.

Obsolete Bulgarian goods have found few buyers outside the former Communist bloc, and some factories have been forced to shut down. Production fell gradually in the early 1990s. Although the government is planning to privatize state-owned companies, many of them remain unprofitable and are attracting little interest from potential buyers.

Agriculture

Collectivization—the reorganization of private farms into large estates under state supervision—transformed Bulgarian

Courtesy of Gordon Rose

Foreign agricultural scientists visit one of Bulgaria's state cooperatives. With hundreds of workers and extensive land holdings, many of the larger cooperatives proved difficult to break up. By 1993, however, the Bulgarian government had succeeded in privatizing most of the country's farmland.

Photo by M. Bryan Ginsberg

A farmer drives his cart through a quiet village.

agriculture in the 1940s and 1950s. Although many Bulgarians resisted the new policy, the government eventually succeeded in collectivizing the land and in setting up a network of large, state-run farming cooperatives.

The Communist regime did allow farmers and city workers to keep small, private plots. These plots proved to be much more productive than state-owned cropland. The government also permitted farmers to sell their surplus produce in local markets, a practice that helped Bulgaria to avoid serious food shortages.

Throughout the 1960s and 1970s, new investment in machinery improved Bulgaria's crop yields. The country's increasing population, however, put a strain on the food supply. At the same time, many peasants were leaving the countryside for jobs in the cities. Bulgarian farmers who

Farm workers painstakingly pick and sort peanuts by hand. Lacking new machinery, many farmers must hire day laborers for planting and harvesting certain crops.

Tractors stand ready for use at a farming cooperative. After World War II, Bulgaria became an important producer of heavy agricultural equipment. Bulgaria exported many of its tractors to the other Communist nations of Europe.

55

Waiting patiently for a nibble on his line, a fisherman sits near the seawall at Varna.

remained on the collectives earned fixed salaries and had little motivation to increase their production.

In the early 1990s, Bulgaria's new government announced plans to end the collective system and to privatize agricultural land. Nevertheless, the state still owns many huge agricultural complexes that are responsible for providing much of the country's food. With their own processing plants and large, integrated operations, these complexes will be difficult to break up and transfer to private owners.

Bulgaria grows most of its grains, including wheat, corn, barley, and rye, on

A wine vendor measures out a sample of his product in a Sofia marketplace.

A tobacco grower has hung leaves out to dry along a city street. Tobacco, which thrives only in warm climates, is one of Bulgaria's most valuable cash crops.

the Danube Plateau. Farmers raise sugar beets for processing into sugar, and sunflowers provide cooking oil and livestock feed. The mild climate of the Thracian Plain supports a wide variety of vegetables and fruits, as well as cotton, rice, and tobacco, which has become the country's most important cash crop.

Vineyards near the Black Sea and on the Thracian Plain produce grapes for Bulgaria's red and white wines. In the Valley of Roses in central Bulgaria, millions of pink and white roses produce a valuable oil, which is distilled into a perfume known as attar of roses. It takes about 250 pounds of rose petals to make a single ounce of attar, a substance that is worth more than gold on world markets.

Mining and Energy

Bulgaria's mining industry provides important raw materials to the country's factories. The iron ore deposits of the Rhodope Mountains supply iron and steel plants, which also use manganese and chromium. Factories process raw copper,

The Iskur Dam is part of a hydroelectric project on the Iskur River, a waterway that flows north through the Balkan Mountains to the Danube. Without major reserves of oil or coal, Bulgaria must rely on hydropower, nuclear plants, and imported energy to generate its electricity.

zinc, and lead ore into finished metals. Bulgarian companies also work small deposits of gold, silver, and uranium.

Lignite (brown coal) from the Maritsa valley and the Sofia region fuels Bulgaria's electrical power plants, although the country's reserves of lignite and anthracite (black coal) are steadily dwindling. Bulgaria also has small stocks of oil and natural gas. Refineries at Burgas and Pleven process crude oil into gasoline and industrial chemicals.

For many years, Bulgaria relied on energy supplies from the Soviet Union, which provided natural gas and other fuels at rates well below world market prices. The collapse of the Communist bloc abruptly ended this trade. Bulgaria's oil and gas fields cannot meet the country's energy needs, and most fuel must now be imported at higher market prices.

Romania and the Soviet Union undertook joint projects to build hydropower stations and nuclear power plants in Bulgaria. The nuclear facility at Kozlodui, one of the largest in the world, generates about 40 percent of the country's electricity. The reactors at Kozlodui have experienced several breakdowns and accidents, and many experts consider the complex to be obsolete and dangerous. Bulgaria, however, lacks the money needed to upgrade the plant.

Foreign Trade

After World War II, Bulgaria linked its trade closely to other nations of the Communist bloc. By the 1980s, Bulgaria was conducting more than 80 percent of its foreign trade with European Communist nations, mostly with the Soviet Union.

Photo by Anne-Marie Hupchick and Dennis P. Hupchick

A fisherman tends his sail in Nesebur. Although many small boats ply the Black Sea, Bulgaria has not developed a large commercial fishing industry.

A Greek truck idles at a gas station. Bulgarian highways are crowded with trucks carrying freight between Europe and the Middle East.

Bags of red peppers line a street in rural Bulgaria, where fertile soil and a warm climate support many kinds of fruits and vegetables. Bulgaria's plentiful food exports have earned the country the nickname "the salad bowl of Europe."

Bulgarian farms exported grain, fruits, and vegetables, and the nation's factories turned out tractors, engines, and other heavy machinery.

To coordinate their economies, the leaders of Communist nations held the prices of these products at artificially low levels. Foreign trade remained an important part of the Bulgarian economy, but without competition to stimulate new investment and innovation, the country's goods were becoming obsolete.

After the breakup of the Communist bloc, Bulgaria's export markets in eastern Europe declined. Germany became Bulgaria's most important trading partner. Imported goods, which the country now had to buy at market prices, became much more expensive, and Bulgarian consumers continued to suffer shortages. To help its foreign trade, the nation is struggling to update its factories to produce goods that meet western European standards.

Bulgaria exports ships, trucks, machinery, and electronic equipment. The nation's fruits and vegetables still have a strong market throughout Europe. Bulgaria also exports large amounts of agricultural fertilizers, as well as tobacco and attar of roses. Metals, fuels, heavy machinery, and electrical equipment are the most common imports.

Transportation

Bulgaria overhauled its road and rail system after World War II to link cities, towns, and Black Sea ports. The Bulgarian railroad system dates to 1866, when the British built a line between the two ports of Ruse and Varna. The Orient Express line, which traveled between western European cities and Istanbul, was later routed through Sofia and the Maritsa valley. The Bulgarian railroads now use 4,000 miles of track and have become the most important means of moving passengers and freight through the country.

Roads extend to smaller towns and villages, where inhabitants use a national bus service. As an important transporta-

tion link between Europe and the Middle East, Bulgaria receives a heavy volume of truck traffic along its major highways. In 1954 engineers completed a road and rail bridge across the Danube, linking Ruse with Giurgiu, Romania.

A small fleet of merchant ships operates out of Varna and Burgas. River barges and cargo and passenger boats also call at Ruse. The state airline, Balkan, flies international and domestic routes from a major airport at Sofia. Other airports have been built in Plovdiv, Varna, Burgas, and Ruse.

Tourism

Travelers visiting Bulgaria enjoy the country's beaches, mountain resorts, cities, and rural villages. The government has built new hotels and resorts to attract more vacationers, whose foreign currency boosts the Bulgarian economy. In the late 1980s,

Courtesy of Gordon Rose

The marble theater at Plovdiv dates to the second century B.C. The largest ancient monument in Bulgaria, the theater still hosts concerts and plays and can seat 3,000 spectators.

Hrelyo's Tower, in the courtyard of the Rila Monastery, was named for Lord Hrelyo. This Bulgarian noble rebuilt the monastery after it was destroyed by avalanches and a fire in the fourteenth century. The tower was the only building to survive another devastating fire at the complex in 1833.

Bulgaria welcomed about 10 million tourists each year, many of them from Turkey, the former republics of Yugoslavia, and the nations that once made up the Soviet bloc. An increasing number of western Europeans arrived in the early 1990s.

Sofia boasts mosques, Orthodox churches, art galleries, and the National History Museum. A summer music festival draws appreciative audiences every year. Architects have restored old homes and churches in the historic Bulgarian capital of Veliko Turnovo. Visitors can explore the ruins of a fortress and a palace at Preslav, a tenth-century capital.

The Rila Monastery in southern Bulgaria was a stronghold of Bulgarian culture during the Turkish occupation, and many fine works of Bulgarian religious art have survived in the monastery's buildings. Near the city of Kazanluk, travelers observe the picking and processing of roses in May and June. Gabrovo, whose residents are famous for their keen sense of humor, hosts a festival of comedy every two years.

Visitors also enjoy summer resorts on the Black Sea coast and skiing vacations on Mount Vitosha near Sofia. The mineral springs of Sandanski, a spa in the Struma

Photo © David and Cathy Memmott

A weaver works at her loom in Veliko Turnovo. Also in the neighborhood are the workshops of skilled potters, jewelers, and goldsmiths, who sell their wares directly to the public in small retail stores.

Courtesy of Susan and Randall Baker

The Alexander Nevsky Memorial Cathedral in Sofia was built in the early twentieth century. Named after a thirteenth-century prince, who saved Russia from an invasion, the church symbolizes the gratitude of Bulgarians for Russia's help in liberating them from the Turks.

River Valley, attract health-conscious people from all over Europe.

The Future

Bulgaria's new leaders have taken important steps to improve the country's economy. The government is planning to sell state-owned companies and to privatize farming collectives. In a country that remained a loyal member of the Soviet bloc for more than 40 years, however, economic change may prove difficult.

Bulgaria still has one of Europe's weakest economies. The nation was unprepared for trade competition, and many firms have cut production and fired workers. Severe unemployment, rising prices, and a drop in living standards has resulted. With limited success, Bulgaria's leaders are trying to attract aid from western Europe and the United States in order to rebuild and modernize important industries.

The problems of economic reform have also caused strife within Bulgarian society, which has led to frequent elections and changes in government. Although most political parties favor the new policies, bitter disagreements have arisen over the speed and methods of reform. If the

Photo © David and Cathy Memmott

Holding freshly picked flowers, Bulgarian children wait for a graduation ceremony to begin.

leaders of Bulgaria can settle their many differences, the nation has a chance to establish a stable economic and political system.

This rural laborer is now working privately held lands and selling his produce for a profit. This change benefits some Bulgarian farmers, but others may fail without state support and without investment in modern machinery.

Photo by Torsten Kjellstrand

Index

949.77
BUL

0 2051 0012860 7

Bulgaria in
pictures.

$16.24

DATE DUE	BORROWER'S NAME	ROOM NO.

0 2051 0012860 7

949.77
BUL

Bulgaria in
pictures.

EMILY DICKINSON LIBRARY
7047 208TH AVE NE, REDMOND, WA

449318 01624   04813A